Gillelan
July 1995

BREAK WRITER'S BLOCK NOW!

BREAK WRITER'S BLOCK NOW!

HOW TO DEMOLISH IT FOREVER
AND
ESTABLISH A PRODUCTIVE WORKING SCHEDULE
IN
ONE AFTERNOON

A Proven System

JERROLD MUNDIS

ST. MARTIN'S PRESS ▪ NEW YORK

BREAK WRITER'S BLOCK NOW! Copyright © 1991 by Jerrold
Mundis. All rights reserved. Printed in the United States of
America. No part of this book may be used or reproduced in any
manner whatsoever without written permission except in the
case of brief quotations embodied in critical articles or reviews.
For information, address St. Martin's Press, 175 Fifth Avenue,
New York, N.Y. 10010

Design by Fearn Cutler

Library of Congress Cataloging-in-Publication Data

Mundis, Jerrold J.
     Break writer's block now! / Jerrold Mundis.
         p.   cm.—(The Writer's library)
     ISBN 0-312-05394-0
        1. Writer's block. I. Title. II Series: Writer's library
(New York, N.Y.)
PN171.W74M86   1991
808′.001′9—dc20   90-21113
                                           CIP

First Edition: April 1991

10 9 8 7 6 5 4 3 2 1

For Jim Mundis, my father,
a newspaper man and a good man
with love

CONTENTS

INTRODUCTION

Writer's block—whether it's over a novel, a dissertation, or a business report—is agony. And wanting to write but not knowing how to fit that desire into the demands of the rest of your life can be painful too. Both conditions are completely unnecessary.

This book will free you from writer's block immediately, and forever: You will never fear or be crippled by it again. Nor will you ever languish under an inability to find the time to write, no matter what your life is like. I know this unequivocally: I've been breaking block for myself for twenty-five years, and for others— while also creating for them a reliable and productive working schedule—for the past five years. And in that time I have written and published:

• Seventeen novels, including *Gerhardt's Children* and *The Dogs*.

• Six books of nonfiction, including *Prelude to Civil War* and *How to Get Out of Debt, Stay Out of Debt & Live Prosperously*.

• Seven film novelizations, including *The Deer Hunter*.

• Some ninety short stories, essays, and articles.

Among my publishers are Atheneum, Arbor House, Delacorte, Bantam, Warner Books, Jove, Berkley, Pocket Books, and New American Library.

My short work has appeared in such publications as *The New York Times Magazine, American Heritage, Harper's Weekly,* the *Magazine of Fantasy & Science Fiction, Glamour,* and *New York* magazine.

My books have been selections of: the Book-of-the-Month Club, Literary Guild, Doubleday Book Club, and Field & Stream Book Club.

My novels have been translated into a dozen foreign languages.

I have taught professional writing and been a consultant editor for *The New York Times.*

I am as vulnerable to writer's block as anyone else, yet the worst I've ever suffered from it has been an occasional afternoon in which I said to hell with it, it's too much of a struggle, and went for a walk with the dog. The reason for this—for not having stared at a blank page in torment or been unable to work for days, weeks, even months, or years—has been the system in this book. That is also the reason I have been able to write steadily through periods of my life in which there were many other demands and claims upon my time.

I developed these concepts and techniques in order to survive: Writing was my sole source of income; I had a wife and children; I couldn't *afford* to be blocked, or to go very long without writing for any other reason.

Early on I was only partly aware that I was formulating and practicing specific techniques. Later I became more conscious and deliberate. The point was, always, simply to be able to continue writing—no matter how I felt or what was happening in my life. And I was. Along the way I occasionally helped others who were blocked or who felt they couldn't begin or continue to write in the face of an increasingly full schedule. Usually that meant an evening going over with them the main points of what I eventually refined into this system.

As time passed, I began to receive requests for this help—sometimes from people I didn't even know, who had got to me through a chain of acquaintances. For a while I didn't mind. But eventually it became a burden, something that was at times even *expected* of me simply because I *could* do it. So I began saying no, and continued saying no for about five years, until the fall of 1985.

I was at a weekend transformational seminar in New York then, the only professional writer among roughly one hundred people. In all, seven individuals approached me to discuss their own writing: Three were blocked, one could find time to write only in fits and starts; of the others, one asked "how" to write, another was seeking an agent, and one wanted me to critique a novel. In as friendly a manner as I could, I told them each that there wasn't much I could do and referred them to a couple of books and a magazine for writers.

One of these people, a woman named Elaine, was a charming, Mississippi-born professor of English at a college in the city. Two years earlier she had been cured of a serious disease through a nontraditional method of healing. She had written about half of a projected three-hundred-page book on the experience, but had now been blocked for more than a year. Politely she asked why I wouldn't help, and was so disarming that I explained.

"Why, darlin'," she said, "then why don't you let me pay you?"

I became embarrassed.

"I pay my dentist," she said. "*I* get paid. You got a hang-up about money, darlin'?"

A month later I taught Elaine how to finish her book—in one three-hour session, for which she paid me. Because of Elaine, I have been breaking block and establishing reliable and productive working schedules for professional and nonprofessional writers for the past five years.

Among the professionals I have helped are a staff writer for the *New Yorker*, a contributor to *Esquire* and other magazines, a playwright and screenwriter, an award-winning novelist, and a nonfiction writer who had been unable to work on a nearly finished novel for eight years. Among the nonprofessionals are graduate and undergraduate students, a psychotherapist, a real-estate salesman, a housewife, an actress, a singer, and a grandmother who wanted to write her memoirs for her family.

It has been fun, and satisfying. But I have been astonished to learn just how many people there are who suffer from block or believe their lives are too busy to allow them to write. Several hundred thousand graduate students alone are unable, year after year, to write their theses or dissertations. As many as one in every three Americans will attempt to write something for publication at some point—and most will either suffer block or give up because of other demands on their time. Many of my clients have urged me to put this service into book form, for people with whom I can't work personally. Finally that seems to me a good idea: I get to write, I get paid, and I get to help—all of which I enjoy.

If you are agonized over block or over not having the time to write, then this book is for you. If you spend about an afternoon with me here, you will never fear or be crippled by writer's block again.

A USER'S GUIDE

This user's guide is designed to help you gain the maximum benefit from the book. Today read only to the end of this section. There are a few preparations it would be best to make before you begin the text proper.

The book is similar to a personal consultation session. The structure is the same, and so is the material it covers. You will need about three to four hours to get through it.

Part I is conceptual: It explains what writer's block is and where it comes from. Part II is practical: It contains the techniques that will enable you to break your block immediately—no matter how powerfully it has gripped you, or for how long—and to establish a reliable and productive working schedule. Both parts are important. Do not be tempted to go directly to the second without reading the first. The best way to work with the book is to follow the seven guidelines below as closely as you can. Doing so will help you get the most out of the book. You'll need a pad and pen when you begin. But before you do that, ideally you will do the following:

1.
READ THE INTRODUCTION.

If you skipped the introduction, go back and read it now. It's important for you to know who I am and where this system comes from.

2.
SELECT A GOOD PLACE TO READ THIS BOOK.

If we were doing this together, you would come to my apartment, which is located in an old Federal building on a narrow, tree-lined street in Greenwich Village, in New York City. I'd show you into my studio, which is a comfortable room that overlooks a quiet courtyard with trees. My desk and working area are here. There is a fireplace on one wall and across from it a couch and a Queen Anne chair, where we would sit. There are bookshelves on the walls and a couple of pieces of art: a large stone lithograph of a terrier, a colored steel engraving of a temple with three statues of Buddha.

Pick a room in which to read this book that is psychologically pleasing to you, in which you feel comfortable and able to relax. If you live in a small studio apartment or a dormitory room, then pick the chair or area that most lends itself to these feelings. If possible, make it a space you also associate with potency or effectiveness in yourself.

3.
SELECT AN APPROPRIATE DAY AND TIME.

Saturday, in the early afternoon, may be a good time. I often schedule consultation sessions then. That gives you time to accomplish a task or two in the morning, if you'd like, but is still early enough for you to feel fresh and alert. The point is to pick a day in which you have no other obligations and a time at which your energy remains high.

4.
ARRANGE TO BE FREE OF INTERRUPTIONS.

It is best to have the time completely to yourself while you work with this book, as free of interruptions as possible. If you have children or pets that need attention, arrange for your spouse or a friend to take them out for the afternoon, if you can. Unplug your phone. Plan on not answering the door. You won't miss anything important. If using your own house or apartment is a problem, then arranging to use a friend's for the afternoon might be a good solution. It is important to have this time as much to yourself as you can.

5.
IF POSSIBLE, READ THE BOOK IN ONE SITTING.

This system can break writer's block and establish a reliable and productive working schedule for you in one afternoon. That's how I designed it, and that's how I use it. A client needs to come to me only once, for a single session. With a few people I've done some telephone follow-up, usually a brief call once a week, for a month or two. But although those people clearly felt better for the extra contact, I doubt they really *needed* it; basically, all I did during those calls was to review with them what they already knew and tinker a bit with their writing schedules. The primary value for them, I think, was in the access to a confident and supportive voice.

Also, each part of this system enhances and builds upon the preceding parts. The effect is cumulative, and so while it is certainly not necessary for you to work through the book in a single afternoon, the system will achieve its maximum impact, and you'll get the biggest benefit from it, if you do.

6.
FOLLOW THE INSTRUCTIONS.

There are only a few exercises for you to do in this book. They are easy and don't take up much time. It is to your benefit to do them, and as they appear. Simply to read through them, thinking they're not relevant or that you'll come back to them later, will destroy their value; you'll only be cheating yourself if you do that.

At intervals, usually at the end of a chapter, I suggest that you pause, take a couple of deep breaths, and relax for a minute or two. Please do. Five years of working with people in person have made it clear where you're likely to need a break, or when you've been concentrating long enough or might be growing physically uncomfortable, or where a transition is useful in order to let an idea settle in before moving on to another.

Finally:

7.

KNOW THAT THIS SYSTEM WORKS—NO MATTER WHO YOU ARE OR WHAT THE CIRCUMSTANCES OF YOUR LIFE.

It has worked for an eighteen-year-old college student and a seventy-two-year-old grandmother; for a professor of economics and an ex-convict who never finished high school; for a busy lawyer, a man who was unemployed, an immigrant for whom English is a second language, and for a single mother who works full time and who, as a member of Alcoholics Anonymous, goes to meetings four or five times a week. In short, it has worked for people from every kind of life imaginable—and it will work for you.

The best thing to do at this point is to close the book and set it aside. If you can arrange things thus, don't open it again until you're settled into a comfortable chair in a pleasing room, on an afternoon in which you are free of interruptions, with a pad and a pen at your side. Then, open to Chapter 1 and begin. Finally, enjoy yourself. This is liberation: You don't ever have to fear or be crippled by writer's block again.

PART

I

THE CONCEPTS

CHAPTER

1

GENTLY

Ideally you've arranged to have this afternoon completely to yourself, free of interruptions, and you're in a comfortable room, in a comfortable chair, feeling fresh and alert. Good. We're ready to begin.

This chapter contains a relaxation exercise. I'd like you to read it through to the end before you actually do it, so you have a full sense of the exercise in mind when you begin. The purpose of the exercise is to clear your mind of its chatter and random thoughts and your body of its unconscious tension, and to leave you feeling fresh and relaxed. It takes about five or six minutes to do.

It's not necessary to memorize anything in this or the following paragraphs—all you need is a general sense of how to do the exercise. After you've read through it and are ready to begin, loosen any part of your clothing that is tight or restricting. Uncross your legs and put your feet flat on the floor. Place your hands on your thighs or in your lap, palms up, in a comfortable position. Close your eyes. Take a deep breath. As you exhale, let your body relax. Let the chair support you. Take another breath, relaxing your body as you exhale.

Now breathe in again, but this time hold the breath. Tense your feet. Keep them tensed for a few moments. Then relax them suddenly; and at the same time, exhale. Repeat the process with your calves: Breathe in, hold the breath, tense your calves, keep them tensed a few moments, then relax them suddenly, and exhale. Repeat the process with your thighs. Then work your way up the rest of your body in this manner, relaxing it part by part: buttocks, belly, chest, shoulders, arms (with wrists and hands), neck, and finishing with your face. After you've done your face, take two easy breaths. Then breathe in one more time, hold that breath, tense your whole body, keep it tensed a few moments, then relax it all at once, and exhale.

Now sit quietly, without tension, and allow the chair to support you. Your breathing may be a little deeper and slower than usual. Gradually become aware of it: . . . in . . . out . . . in . . . out. Don't think about it, analyze it, or try to change it: Just be aware of it. Then gently, very gently, begin to focus on it, as best you can, to the exclusion of everything else: . . . in . . . out . . . in . . . out. You'll probably be distracted by other awarenesses or random thoughts. That's perfectly normal. Don't try to force them out of your mind, which doesn't work. Instead, when you become aware of an intruding thought, simply let it drift across your consciousness, like a cloud across the sky, and disappear, then gently return your focus to your breathing: . . . in . . . out . . . in . . . out. Two or three minutes of this easy focus is enough.

When you're done, keep your eyes closed a few moments longer, allowing yourself to be still. Then move your hands a little, shift your feet on the floor. Let your eyes open, slowly. After a few moments, stretch, take a couple of good breaths, and stretch again. When you're ready, pick up the book and turn to the next chapter. Okay? Good. Now set the book down and do the exercise.

CHAPTER

2

THE MOVING PEN

Welcome back. Feels good, doesn't it? This and the following chapter each contain another exercise. They are the last two in Part 1 of the book. This one shouldn't require more than three or four minutes to do. You'll need your pad and pen. As in the last chapter, read through the exercise before you do it.

When you're ready to begin, write this sentence on the first line of your pad: "I am years gone from my family and miles away."

Then write something after it, anything at all. The point of the exercise—the *only* point—is to keep your pen moving. Don't stop to think. It doesn't matter what you put down, whether it's literate or illiterate, makes sense or not. That's irrelevant. The only point is to keep your pen moving. Don't worry about what's on the page; no one is ever going to see it.

While you're doing this, remind yourself that *what* you put down doesn't matter, the point is just to keep the pen moving. The words can be any kind, in any form—a piece of a letter, a journal entry, notes, a stream of consciousness, even a description of last night's dinner. Anything at all. The only point is to keep the pen moving. After three or four minutes of this, whatever feels comfortable, finish the thought or sentence you're on, or the next one if you want, and put a period there. The exercise is over.

Got it? Good. Do the exercise.

When you're finished, set your pen and pad down, take a deep breath, and relax. Stretch. Take another breath, and then go on to the next chapter. But remember, do the exercise first.

CHAPTER

3

TELL ME WHY

Congratulations! You're not blocked. You have just proved that you are free of any physical condition that would prevent you from writing: You have no organ failure, no inability to hold a pen. You put words on paper. So it must be something else.

Let's do a discovery process here. Turn to a fresh page on your pad. Across the top write: "A reason I can't write is:" Below that list the numbers 1 through 12. Take a couple of breaths and relax. Say aloud to yourself, "A reason I can't write is . . ." Then write down the first thing that comes to mind next to number 1. Say again, "A reason I can't write is . . ." And again put down the first thing that springs to mind. Do this without pause until you've come up with twelve answers.

If you get stuck, just make one up and go on. There are no right or wrong answers here, only the answers you have. It's important to keep the flow going, one answer after another without hesitation, without stopping to say "Well, let me see . . . uh . . ."

When you're finished, take a couple of deep breaths. Stand up and stretch. Move your shoulders. Shake your arms if you feel like it. Stretch once more, take another couple of breaths. Then sit down again, get comfortable, and go on to the next chapter.

4

YOU AND EVERYONE ELSE

Did you discover any surprises in that last exercise? Many people do, or at least find that they put into words for the first time some thoughts of which they were only vaguely, and uncomfortably, aware. No one ever comes up with precisely the same set of reasons as anyone else, but nearly everyone does share a fair number with others who are blocked. Among those that appear the most frequently are:

- I'm afraid it won't be published.

- I don't want to write another book that gets badly reviewed [or that doesn't make enough money].

- It won't be as good as I think it should be.

- I'm afraid my friends won't like it.

- My family will be angry with me if I write truthfully.

- I'll never have the energy to finish it.

- My ideas seem trivial.

- I'm concerned over form—I don't want to spend years learning it.

- I'm surrounded by people who judge only by results.

- I don't have the time.

- I grow anxious when I do it.

- It's not a "proper" activity, not productive like holding a job or cleaning the house.

- I have so many projects I don't know which one to start on.

- I'll never be as successful as I want, so why try?

- I'll expose myself. I won't be able to hide any more.

- It isn't "real."

- I don't have the discipline.

- My family and friends will be jealous if I'm successful.

- If I do it regularly, I'll have to isolate, and I'm afraid of that.

- I don't have enough confidence.

- I'd have to give up too much.

- I'm afraid of success.

- When it's not perfect it drives me crazy.

- I don't have the inspiration.

- There's too much else to do.

- It won't produce the money I need.

- I don't have anything to say anymore.

- It's too competitive.

- No one will understand me.

- I'm burned out.

- I'm unstructured and disorganized.

- I've been doing it for years and I'm just sick and tired of it.

How many of your own answers were reflected here? Sometimes it's a relief simply to know that you're not alone, that there is nothing weird or unique about you. There are other reasons given, of course, and of those many are specific to the individual—"I've got two children under five" (which is actually only another way of saying "I don't have enough time"). But the ones just listed are cited repeatedly and are among the most potent.

For now, don't concern yourself with your answers. We'll address them in later chapters. Here the point is simply for you to be aware of them and to know that they don't differ much from those of others who are blocked.

Take a couple of breaths. Stretch and relax. Make yourself comfortable, and turn to the next chapter.

CHAPTER

5

WHAT IT IS

I'm going to tell you what writer's block is:

It's a myth.
There is no such thing.

Block does not exist. It is not real. There is no organ failure, no inability to hold a pen. There is no man with a gun threatening to blow your brains out if you write.

Writing is a simple act. It is no more "magical" than painting a board, washing a window, or throwing a ball. Writing is the simple act of putting words on paper. That's all. You proved in Chapter 2 that you can do that—you put words on paper. So you are not really "blocked": You can perform the simple act of putting words on paper.

"But . . . !"

That's okay. I know how you feel. Take a really deep breath here. Let it out, then turn to the next chapter.

6

I THINK, THEREFORE I AM

"Block" is wholly in your mind. It is a *choice* not to write, not an *inability*. It is a choice made in response to your cognitions—your thoughts and beliefs—and nearly always masked by excuses, by "reasons" such as those you listed in Chapter 3. The same is true of not having enough time to write, which is simply another form of block, albeit a subtle one.

Your subconscious accepts every conscious thought or belief you have as literal truth. One of its major functions is to prove the validity of our thoughts. This helps us stay sane. Let's say, to illustrate, that I believe: "Life sucks." If, in the face of this belief, I continually run into people who are glad to see me, if my work is praised and respected, if I am loved and valued by family and friends, then I won't stay sane very long—because my experiences will directly contradict my belief structure, and that is an untenable position for anyone. So something must change here.

You'd think that I would resolve the conflict by changing my belief to reflect my experience, wouldn't you? That I'd start thinking: "Life is pretty nice." But rarely do we do that. Instead, what nearly always happens is that our subconscious will arrange for us to experience only what will support and prove our beliefs, what we *think*. Without even being aware of what I'm doing, I'll take other streets where I won't encounter people who are glad to see me, or be too rushed or tired to smile back at them, I'll become sloppy or late with my work, critical of and impatient with the people who love me. And as a result, my experiences will begin to support my belief again.

If my thought, or belief, is "I'm blocked. I can't write," then my subconscious will dutifully provide me with the appropriate experience. That's its job.

But what about the "reasons" on your list? At least *some* of those are real, aren't they? You *do* have two kids and a full-time job. An absolute statement of fact is indeed real. And that you have two children and a job is a fact; but the statement you formulate because of that fact—"I don't have enough time"—is a *belief*. "It will never be published" is a belief.

What is "enough" time?

How can you *know* it will never be published?

Recognizing beliefs for what they are—simply beliefs—is a major step forward. You don't need months or years of therapy to overcome them. You'll have done that by the time you finish this book. Even if some remain strongly entrenched within you, you'll still be able to write, despite their presence, by using the techniques in the second part of the book.

Anyone can write at any time—even in the face of crushing

neurosis, anxiety, depression, self-doubt. Franz Kafka is witness to this. So are Louis-Ferdinand Céline, the Marquis de Sade, Emily Dickinson, F. Scott Fitzgerald, Virginia Woolf, Sylvia Plath, Ezra Pound, even Woody Allen, and the litany of others who have written despite acute psychological difficulties. This is not to suggest that writers are a troubled lot or that literary accomplishment springs from neurosis. They aren't, and it doesn't. But it is to say that regardless of what's going on in your mind, there is no reason for you to be blocked.

I have and have always had my own "reasons," which probably don't differ much from yours. But I have written steadily anyway, even through periods of great stress and upheaval, including a divorce, illness, and bouts of financial pressure. There was no great trick in that, only the system in this book. Now, nothing says that anyone *should* write during such periods. It may even be desirable not to. But the point is, even then, we can write if we wish to. Writing, remember, is a simple act—nothing more than putting words on paper.

This is a good place to take a couple of breaths, stretch, and relax for a minute or two before going on.

CHAPTER

7

MYTHS

There are many myths about writers. These myths are mostly harmless, except when writers themselves believe them; then they can contribute to block. Let's examine the most common and destructive ones.

WRITERS ARE CONSUMMATE MASTERS OF THE LANGUAGE.

No, they're not. Most aren't even qualified to teach a high school grammar course. They may once have been able to define the parts of speech and rules of syntax, but the majority couldn't do so now. More write by "feel" for the rules than conscious knowledge of them.

You doubt that? As an experiment, I got out of my chair after writing the last paragraph and took down from the shelf a classic reference work, the *Harbrace Handbook of English*. I opened it to the table of contents (nineteen pages long), in order to see how many entries I could run through before coming upon one I couldn't explain. I stopped on the fourth entry: "The Appositive."

The *what*?

Now, I know that "apposite" means appropriate, and that "apposition" means side by side, but that's as far as I go. Here is *Harbrace*'s definition, as it appears in the first chapter: "A substantive set beside another substantive and denoting the same person or thing."

Terrific. What does *that* mean?

Basically, I learned from further explanation on page 25, it means, in proper usage, that you shouldn't write in sentence fragments, that you shouldn't write something like: "It's a big city. Sprawling. Tough. Violent."

Rather, according to *Harbrace*, you should write: "It's a big city; sprawling, tough, violent."

Which would be fine. But so, depending on how you "felt" your material, the tone or mood you were trying to establish, would the first example.

And so would: "It's a big city—sprawling and tough. Violent."

And: "It's a *big* city. Sprawling, tough, and violent."

And: "Big city. Sprawling. Tough. Violent."

Or: "Sprawling, tough, violent: It's a big city."

It all depends on what you're after. Other listings in Harbrace that baffled me were: "Correction by co-ordination," "Pronouns used as predicate complements," "Simple futurity," and "Subjunctive Mood: Wishes or Regrets, Concessions, etc." My bafflement in the face of these, however, has not prevented me from publishing thirty books; nor did it stop the Literary Guild and Book-of-the-Month Club from selecting my work for their members.

Every writer, of course, needs to be familiar with at least basic grammar, to know the difference, for example, between a noun and a verb, an adjective and an adverb, or to understand number agreement. (Understanding the latter, even if you couldn't define it, means that you would write "Frank is a cop in Detroit," rather than "Frank are a cop in Detroit.")

While some writers are indeed expert on the formalities of language, most are not. That is why publishers employ editors and copy editors; and even they need to consult reference works. The editors of *The New York Times*, for example, refer constantly to that paper's manual of style and usage, which is 229 pages long. In it, more than a page and a half are devoted solely to the proper use of the apostrophe, which doesn't necessarily reflect the *correct* ways to use the apostrophe, but rather the ways *The New York Times* likes to use it. Other publications have their own preferences.

Continuing the myths:

THEY'RE GENIUSES.

This is flattering. If I weren't writing a book on block, I'd be tempted to let it stand. But the truth is that some writers are highly intelligent, most are about average, and some are a bit below. Dante was a genius, T.S. Eliot an intellectual. But Jacqueline Susann and Mickey Spillane are also accounted writers. Nor does a writer have to be particularly well educated to write. Some hold Ph.D.'s; others never finished high school; most lie somewhere in between. Shakespeare had little formal education. Ben Jonson, one of his contemporaries and a vastly better educated man, said of him that he had "small Latin and less Greek." Shakespeare, however, kept writing. How many of Ben Jonson's plays do you remember?

THEY SIT DOWN AND THE WORDS JUST FLOW.

Wrong. What usually happens is: They write a few words, a sentence, a paragraph or two. Then they scratch their heads or look out the window. They get up and walk around. They check the mail. They play with their calculators. One novelist I know goes so far as to deal himself a hand of solitaire. Then they write another few words, a paragraph or two. Then they scratch their heads, look out the window, get up and walk around. . . .

It's a rare occasion when the words just flow without interruption. More often they flow for thirty seconds, five or ten minutes at a time. Then you stop and think, stare at the page or the screen, look out the window, or whatever it is that you do, and then write for another thirty seconds, five or ten minutes. Once in a while, you'll catch fire and in a white heat type as fast as you can for an hour or two, even three or four. That has happened to me—maybe ten or fifteen times over the past twenty-five years. For most writers, nearly every day it's a matter of hills and valleys, with pauses in between.

INSPIRATION IS THE SOURCE OF THEIR WORK.

Actually, the opposite is true: It's the act of *writing* that causes the *inspiration*. Just as the act of exercise causes high energy and good muscle tone, rather than the other way around.

If I had waited to be inspired before I wrote, my life's work would now amount to about one essay, a couple of short stories, a chapter or two of a nonfiction book, and a few scenes from various novels. If every professional writing today had waited, there would be no professionals writing today. If writers throughout history had waited, the world's body of literature would now fit into a good-size closet.

Am I saying there is no such thing as inspiration? No. There certainly is. But I am saying that to wait for it before you write is to put the cart before the horse. First you write; *then* the inspiration comes. Writers—like athletes or surgeons, mathematicians or musicians—go to work first; the inspiration comes second. The more you write, the more you will be inspired. Not the other way around.

THEY "HAVE IT"—A NATURAL, FULL-BLOWN TALENT.

Right. Just like Linda Ronstadt and Placido Domingo "had it"— spectacular, fully developed talents—from the moment they first opened their mouths to sing. Or Joe Namath and Joe Montana from the moment they first picked up a football. Or Vladimir Horowitz and Pablo Casals the first time they sat down to play their instruments. Or Ernest Hemingway and Eugene O'Neill the first time they put words on paper. No, what each of these had was a *desire* to do what, in time, they came to do so well; and the *potential* for doing it. They nurtured and strengthened that potential, they practiced, improved upon, and finally perfected it, by *doing*.

For a writer, that means by writing. No one begins at the height of his or her powers. In fact, the early work of most writers is inferior, sometimes abysmally so, to their work of later periods— even when that early work was perfectly fine in itself. Just as important to know is that not every piece, even from the same period, will be of uniform quality. Some are simply better than others. Does Dwight Gooden pitch equally well in every game? Are each of Mikhail Baryshnikov's *pas de deux* the match of his others? Not even the best of writers can pull it off every time. Thomas Mann, Edgar Allen Poe, F. Scott Fitzgerald, and anyone else you can think of wrote some real bombs. So have I, and every other writer I know.

WRITERS ARE "DIFFERENT."

Yes, they are. So are bus drivers, plumbers, accountants, dentists, hairdressers, and business executives. What's different about writers is that they write, and other people don't. What's different about bus drivers is that they drive buses, and other people don't.

If you prick a writer, does he not bleed? Writers set the alarm clock at night, they worry about money, have religious and sexual preferences, raise children, get into arguments, grieve, laugh, clean the bathroom, need to get their cars fixed and their laundry done. There is nothing "different" about a writer, no more than there is about anyone who performs an activity that most other people don't. He or she may be more interested in words, stories, or ideas than other people—as a painter is probably more interested in color and shape than other people—but the fundamental difference is that a writer writes, and other people do not.

WRITING IS ECSTASY.

Now and then it is, just as listening to music can be, or dancing, working out, sitting under a night sky, or nearly any other activity that is meaningful to you. And those are tremendous moments. But they are not daily moments. Usually writing is just the simple act of putting words on paper. Sometimes it's harder, sometimes easier; sometimes it's more satisfying, sometimes less so. Ecstasy, anywhere, is an uncommon event.

WRITERS SUFFER.

Some do, some don't. The proportion is about the same as it is for the general population. This idea is on a par with the notion that writers are intensely sensitive or that to create is to know agony. These are fictions promulgated largely by dilettantes who want to be admired or to pick someone up at a party.

What really happens is that when it's a writer who's suffering—rather than, say, an accountant—that suffering may well end up on a printed page where, instead of being known just to a friend or two, a few thousand or hundred thousand people will learn all about it, in poignantly rendered detail. The visibility is higher, that's all.

Pause here. Look up from the book, take a breath, and relax. Now scan the list again, and realize that these are not facts about writers, but simply mistaken *beliefs*. There is no reality to them.

CHAPTER

8

BIG KILLER #1

There are three Big Killers involved in writer's block. Any single one can be deadly. When combined, you don't have a chance against them. The first is:

PERFECTIONISM

Here the underlying thought is: "If it's not perfect, it's worthless." If it's not an A+, it's a failure. If I don't blow the editor out of his chair, I blow the piece. If it doesn't bring the *New York Review of Books* to its knees, it's junk. Perfectionism is an all-or-nothing attitude; and ruled by it, you will nearly always end up with nothing.

Perfection, in any human endeavor, cannot be achieved. Everything ever written, from *The Iliad* to *Humboldt's Gift*, from yesterday's newspaper to your department chairman's groundbreaking book of criticism, could in some way have been made better: by replacing a word, deleting a modifier, repunctuating a sentence, restructuring a paragraph, elaborating a theme, recasting a scene, eliminating a subplot, or in some other fashion. There is no absolute standard. Get ten writers to submit ten changes each for any piece of work ever published, and the majority of a panel of critics—or average readers, for that matter—will agree that at least some of those changes would improve the work.

If you try to write a perfect piece, you are doomed to failure. And why, if you are certain to fail, would you even try? Sophocles could not have written under such a condition. Jackie Collins could not. Neither can you.

Another, more subtle form of perfectionism is to say to yourself something like "In the face of Shakespeare, Tolstoy, Mann, Melville, Faulkner, and all the others, what's the use?" Good point. Since the giants have all been there before you, there's no sense in even trying. You might as well junk your typewriter and start looking for a good dental school.

But Shakespeare could have said, "In the face of Sophocles, what's the use?" And Ibsen could have said, "In the face of Shakespeare, what's the use?" And O'Neill could have said, "In the face of Ibsen, what's the use?" And Tennessee Williams could have said, "In the face of O'Neill, what's the use?" And David Mamet could have said, "In the face of Tennessee Williams, what's the use?" And some playwright whose first work is opening Off-Broadway or in a regional theater tonight could have said, "In the face of David Mamet, what's the use?" And none of them would ever have written.

Perfectionism also manifests in the belief that the work must be excellent the moment you put it on paper. This is simply not true. First drafts frequently bear only a passing resemblance to final drafts. For most writers, the real work takes place in the revision or editing. Brendan Gill, for example, long a writer for the *New Yorker* and known for the elegance of his prose, puts his work through as many as eighteen drafts before he's satisfied with it. Flaubert spent five years reworking *Madame Bovary*, more than twenty years on *The Temptation of St. Anthony*. These are extremes, but they make the point: Very few writers produce finished copy on their first attempt.

In my early twenties, I wrote two or three first-draft books. Still, there were strikeovers on the pages, and when I read through the manuscripts before delivering them to the publisher, I invariably made other changes. Quickly I gave up that manner of working: It was too limiting and it generated too much tension.

Among the novelists I know, three are generally said to be first-draft writers: Lawrence Block, Thomas M. Disch, and Robert Silverberg. Yet each has thrown out ten- and twenty-page chunks in the midst of composition, each pencil-edits his work, typing over heavily marked pages, and each has later done revisions at the request of his editor, sometimes substantial amounts.

My own manner of working (and the one common to most writers) is to get it all down first, no matter how rough, and edit later. Sometimes it's very rough: a stab at a metaphor, an overdone paragraph, a clunker of an image, a labyrinth of a sentence. Also, because I want more than enough to work with rather than too little, I usually overwrite by about 20 percent, which means that I'll cut a first draft of five hundred pages down to about four hundred by the time I'm done.

To illustrate the kind of revision most writers put their work through, here are three pages pulled at random from one of my own novels, *The Dogs* (which first appeared under the pseudonym Robert Calder). The original prose—beneath my pencil-editing— is first draft. The altered version is what appeared in the published book. *The Dogs* was written in pre-computer days; nowadays I do most of my editing on the screen, and no record like this exists.

drank his coffee. it circled restlessly around the table and gave him a small sharp barks, as if it were expecting something.

Bauer looked through the lost and found columns of the Covington Freeman. The pup wasn't listed. In the phone directory under veterinarians, he found a Dr. E.V. Collier on the near side of Covington. He put the pup in the car and drove in.

The doctor was a woman, the E was for Elizabeth. She was thirtyish, oval-faced, with shoulder-length dark blonde hair and grey eyes. She wore a crisp white medical jacket unbuttoned over a skirt and sweater. Bauer had to wait an hour.

"You really should have called for an appointment," she said when she summoned him into the examining room. "Hi, pup," she said to the dog.

"Sorry. I didn't know."

"Well now you do." Her receptionist was out sick and she was growing irritable handling everything alone. She poised a pen over an index card. "Your name, please." She took his address and phone number. "Name and age of your dog?"

"I don't know. I found him. I just wanted to have him checked, find out what kind of shots he should have, get some feeding information."

She sighed and laid the card and pen down. "Okay. Put him up on the table."

Mark ran in. "Mommy there's a dog outside!"

Eileen set aside the spackling knife and wiped her hands on her jeans. "Where, honey?" Mark was four, and overly excitable. She didn't want to send him into hysterics.

She and John had warned him about dogs last week, after that terrible incident with the McPhee boy in Marbleville, which wasn't far. For two days after, he'd refused to go outside without one of them with him.

"Well," John had said, "I'd rather have it this way than have him think there's nothing to it. He'll balance it in a couple of days."

John was legitimately concerned. He was a town constable, and he'd seen animals and livestock that had been killed by feral and night-roaming dogs, and he'd shot two wild ones last winter that were tearing apart a crippled deer.

No ¶ He'd instructed Eileen clearly and unequivocally, and she, who had been raised in the mountains, was not a vacillating

The toothed chain rocketed ~~the chain spun blurrily~~ around the edges of the bar.

The dog ~~turned from j Stokes,~~ lunged against the trap. Stokes ~~got to his feet and advance.~~ advanced. He revved the saw in bursts, showing his white even teeth. Bone ~~splinters~~ poked through the raw flesh of the dog's leg, where the trap had bit. ~~~~ Unable to escape, the ~~dog~~ animal twisted back to face Stokes. Its muzzle wrinkled up and it skinned its lips back from its teeth. Stokes set his ~~~~ legs and pressed the trigger down. The saw screamed. ~~His right x hand was on the grip, his left grasped the support handle.~~ In a unified motion, he threw one foot forward to take his weight, ~~half~~ he crouched and ~~extended his arms and~~ swung the saw in an arc from left to right. The dog bit at it. Its tongue and lower jaw ~~was~~ were ripped apart in a spray of blood and teeth. The dog went over backward ~~only a shred of jaw remaining.~~ It thrashed upright again to face ~~William~~ Stokes. Its eyes were insane. Stokes ~~checked~~ doubled the ~~swing of the~~ saw back. ~~and doubled it back.~~ The animal threw itself away, nearly pulling its broken leg apart. Stokes went after it. The saw chewed into ~~~~ the back of ~~the dog's~~ its skull—and ~~Stokes~~ Stokes's neck exploded in fire. ~~and~~ he was knocked sprawling ~~down.~~

The grey bitch had reached the chicken first. ~~It tried to flee her wing,~~ It squawked and beating its wings and jumped in a circle. The bitch went after it. ~~and~~ Something ~~had~~ erupted from the ground. ~~and~~ It seized her leg and she fell yowling. The spotted dog leapt past her and killed the chicken. The ~~~~ bitch twisted around biting at the thing that held her leg. Orph charged and bit

In a library, look at the manuscripts or manuscript facsimiles of well-known and respected writers. See for yourself the kind of revision and editing they do on their own first drafts. Many of Henry James's pages, for example, are rife with changes; the first draft of T.S. Eliot's *The Wasteland* is marked by Ezra Pound with innumerable suggestions for revision, most of which Eliot incorporated in the final draft.

Perfectionism, no matter what its guise, equals paralysis. Your work doesn't have to be perfect. In fact, it *can't* be. So let go of perfectionism; it is simply not obtainable, by you or anyone else.

This is a good place to set the book down, breathe, and relax for a few moments.

9

BIG KILLER #2

The second of the three Big Killers, which is more a product of the other two rather than an independent element, is:

FEAR

In writer's block, nearly all fear can be reduced to a single statement: "That I can't do it." Therefore, runs the result, you won't do it. Block, as we have pointed out, is a *choice*, not an inability. All "it" is, is the simple act of putting words on paper, remember? And anyone can do that. You may *choose* not to do so, but you are perfectly capable of it.

But I couldn't possibly be Stephen King, you might say. Or Saul Bellow. You are quite right. And they couldn't possibly be Mickey Spillane or Henry James. And Laurie Colwin couldn't possibly be Margaret Atwood, or Joyce Carol Oates be Janet Dailey. No one can be anyone else. Or write like anyone else. Saul Bellow could not write a Stephen King novel if he tried. You can write only like yourself, as best you can, and in a manner natural to your own personality.

To a large degree, merit is a matter of taste rather than fact. A writer may be revered and then ignored within the span of a generation. Hardly anyone who doesn't have to reads a novel by Theodore Dreiser or John Dos Passos these days, though both were once household names. One critic may celebrate a book and another damn it for precisely the same qualities. John Cheever's fans think he is a better writer than Robert B. Parker. Robert B. Parker's fans think he is a better writer than John Cheever. Cynthia Ozick's readers prefer her to Anne Tyler, and Anne Tyler's prefer her to Cynthia Ozick. John Updike says he will be happy if his books remain on the library shelves ten years. Danielle Steel and Marianne Wiggins could scarcely write more differently from one another, yet each banks large royalty checks. And none could write a book like any of the others that would be more than a poor imitation.

Fears, like beliefs, are nearly always self-fulfilling. The subconscious "Prover" comes into play. I'm afraid I can't write. So I don't write. Presto: the fear has fulfilled itself.

BIG KILLER #3

The third Big Killer is:

THE BAGGAGE TRAIN

The Baggage Train is composed of all the reasons you want to write, all the things you wish to accomplish with your writing. Some typical examples follow.

I want to get rich.

I want to be admired.

I want to be on the front page of the *Times Book Review*, the cover of *People* magazine.

I need the money for next month's rent.

I want to get my degree.

I want to enlighten the world.

I want to be immortal.

I want to make everyone laugh and cry.

I want to show them how sensitive I am.

I want all my ex-lovers to say, Boy, I should have stayed with her.

With all these chained to you, one after the other, stretching off into the distance like a great baggage train, you're not going to get very far. You may never even get out of the station. Because you're not sitting down on a Monday morning to write for three hours—you're sitting down to become rich, to become famous, to enlighten the world, to get your degree. And you cannot possibly do that. You cannot become rich sitting in front of your typewriter from nine to twelve on Monday morning. You cannot get your degree, become famous or enlighten the world.

If Tolstoy had sat down and said, "Today I am going to write world literature," he would have slumped over his desk paralyzed with fear. The items on the preceding list, or others like them, may motivate you, may be your underlying reasons for wanting to write (and that's fine); but you *cannot* accomplish a single one of them on any given day. All you *can* accomplish is that day's work, the simple act of putting words on paper. Nothing else is possible.

The point, then, is to uncouple the Baggage Train. When you sit down to write, separate yourself from it and leave it behind you. *Your only task, the only thing you wish to accomplish, the only thing you* can *accomplish, is the simple act of putting words on paper.* Whether they strike you as good, bad, or indifferent (and you're not really fit to judge at the moment) is irrelevant. So is any future result. The only thing you wish to do, the only thing you *can* do, is put words on paper. The goal begins with that, and ends with that.

This brings to a close Part I, the conceptual part of the book. Part II deals with technique. Before you move on to it, I suggest that you take a five-minute break, especially if you have been reading in one sitting. Set the book aside. Stand up. Breathe. Stretch. Relax. Do a couple of big full-body stretches or touch your toes a few times. Make yourself a cup of coffee or get a glass of soda, water, or fruit juice. Do *not* check the answering machine or look to see if the mail has come. Just stay relaxed. When you're ready, sit back down, take a conscious breath or two, and begin reading again.

THE TECHNIQUES

11

THE FOUNDATION

The techniques in this and the following chapters are powerful: practiced in themselves, even without any knowledge of the nature and cause of block, they are often sufficient to demolish it; practiced with such knowledge, they cannot fail to free you and to enable you to write on a reliable and productive schedule.

They are given in five groups: Foundation, Soft, Firm, Hardcore, and Atom Bomb. Each group is important and builds upon what preceded it, as Part II of the book builds upon Part I. If you opened directly to this chapter and haven't read Part I or done the exercises there, then stop, go back, and begin on the first page; you will only handicap yourself otherwise. If you have read the book from the beginning, fine; pause, take a breath, stretch, relax, and continue. This is how you lay the foundation:

1.
THE ONLY GOAL IS TO WRITE.

Remember: The goal of any given day is simply to write. Not to get rich, become famous, save the world, or anything else, but simply to write. Take other considerations, such as marketing, revision, whatever, later. Today the object is nothing more than to put words on paper. Keep this in mind every time you sit down to write.

2.
READ.

You can't write in a vacuum. No more than you can play music if you've never heard it or don't listen to it. So read. And read what you like, not what you think you ought to, whether that's western novels or semiotics. If you don't enjoy your reading, you'll resent it, and sooner or later—usually much sooner—you won't do it at all.

3.
BE CLEAR ABOUT WHAT YOU WANT TO WRITE.

Be clear about what you want to write: poem, short story, essay, novel, memoir, whatever else. A vague desire to write, without any specific focus, is no more effective than a vague desire to travel, without any specific destination. Unless you know where you want to go, you will never get there.

(If you're a graduate student you already know what you want to write. The major problems are usually Perfectionism and the Baggage Train. "If it's not utterly innovative and brilliant," you tell yourself, "it's worthless." Nor are you sitting down to write: You're sitting down to win your degree or establish a career. Which you simply can't do on a given morning. What you *can* do is perform the simple act of putting words on paper.)

Most of the time, you're better off writing what you most like to read. If you enjoy romance novels, you'll have more fun writing a romance novel (and therefore an easier time of it) than you would trying to write a hardboiled crime novel. And since you know more about them, you'll probably do a better job.

4.
WRITE ABOUT WHAT YOU KNOW.

For as long as there have been writing classes, instructors have been telling students to write about what they know. It doesn't take much reflection to see why. An unmarried male attorney who works out on Nautilus equipment doesn't know enough about the thoughts, emotions, experiences, and details of the life of a housewife with young children to write about them convincingly. So also with a female academic trying to write about a biker who never got past the sixth grade and spent half his life in prisons.

For our purposes, there's an even more pressing reason: Ignorance and uncertainty are an invitation to block. Don't try to write about a setting, subject, or character unless you're familiar with it or know how to do effective research. Writing about what you know makes the act of writing much easier.

5.
FELLOW TRAVELERS.

Subscribe to *Writer's Digest*, a magazine pitched largely to beginning writers. Reading it provides a supportive sense of contact with others who are actively engaged with writing. (So does taking a writing class at a nearby college, attending a writer's conference, or belonging to a local writer's group.) Some of the magazine's articles are helpful, and the market information, practical in its own right, may trigger ideas for stories or articles that might otherwise never have occurred to you.

The rest of this chapter comprises what are more supplemental points than actual techniques. However, they are useful to keep in mind.

THE MARKETS.

Marketing is irrelevant to any day's writing. All that *is* relevant is the simple act of putting words on paper. But it is sometimes helpful, particularly for newer writers, to have a sense of how large the market for writing actually is.

There are literally thousands of markets. The possibilities extend far beyond the handful of famous magazines such as the *New Yorker* and *Playboy* or the dozen or so publishing giants such as Doubleday and Random House. For short work, there are perhaps as many as 3,500 publications, ranging from *Esquire* all the way down through trade magazines, sports and hobby journals, regional publications, small literary magazines and the feature departments of local newspapers, to such magazines as *Psychic Guide* and *Room of One's Own*, a feminist publication. For books, there are some 500 potential publishers, from Bantam Books down through the university presses to houses such as Applezaba Press in Long Beach, California, and Eakin Publications in Austin, Texas. The point is simply for you to be aware that there are a great many potential markets.

THERE ARE MANY FORMS OF WRITING.

Realize too that there are many forms of writing beyond the familiar ones like the short story and novel. Regularly published in large numbers are: book, dance, and theater reviews, brochures, how-to columns, local histories, industrial promotions, annual reports, newsletters, and travel and restaurant guides. People also write comedy routines, audiovisual scripts, public relations copy, direct-mail packages, speeches, greeting card verses, and other material.

Now, you may have no interest in most of these. Fine. Neither do I. But it's helpful to know that writing is not limited to three or four possible forms. Only recently, more than twenty years after I first began to publish, did it occur to me that I might enjoy writing book reviews. I tried it, found out that I did, and now write them occasionally.

REJECTIONS ARE (NEARLY) MEANINGLESS.

A piece may be rejected for any one of dozens of reasons that have nothing to do with its quality. An editor who just discovered that her husband is having an affair will probably not look with favor on your feature about the illicit pleasures of infidelity. Or a magazine may have published a story similar to yours a month or two ago. Or a piece is perfectly good, but you picked the wrong market. *Glamour*'s readers, for example, are a median age of twenty-seven; they are not interested in reading about how to cope with the empty-nest syndrome. *Playboy* publishes only 20 some short stories a year, yet each year it receives 25,000 submissions. Or your style simply might not be to the taste of a particular editor.

In each of these situations, your manuscript—while possibly very good, and welcome at another market—will be rejected. This not only happens to beginners, but to Joyce Carol Oates and Isaac Bashevis Singer as well.

In my case, the most celebrated novel I ever published, *Gerhardt's Children*, was rejected by an editor who said he just didn't care for that kind of book, then by another who called it "highly pretentious," and was then bought by a third, who called it one of the best novels he'd read in the last ten years. The book was later selected by the Book-of-the-Month Club and published to highly praising reviews. So what did those first two rejections mean? Only that the book did not appeal to those two editors.

In themselves, then, rejections tell you very little about the merit of your work—usually. There are exceptions. The first is this: If everything you have ever written (assuming a reasonable body of work, say a minimum of three or four books, or ten to fifteen short pieces) has been repeatedly rejected by market after market, there may be a fundamental flaw in your work; which might or might not be easy to correct. Either way, you need professional help. Get a critique—not from a teacher, a friend in advertising or public relations, or even someone who specializes in critiques, but from a working writer or editor, someone who earns his or her living that way.

The second exception is the positive rejection: from which something can be learned, or that compliments some aspect of your work, invites you to submit other material, or asks you to rework this manuscript and submit it again. Editors are busy people who have to deal with hundreds of manuscripts. They do not have the time to write even single-line notes to writers they think are un-talented or incapable. So when they do write, it is meaningful. Pay attention to such communications. There is usually something for you to learn from them. And follow up on any requests from an editor—they are not made lightly.

It's time to pause again. Breathe. Relax for a few moments, then go on.

12

SOFT TECHNIQUES

There are three techniques in this chapter. The first and last are exercises that are to be done here, while reading the book. The middle one, which you can begin at a later date, is an ongoing process that will serve you well for years.

1.

WHAT TO DO WITH THE PRACTICAL REASONS.

Turn to a fresh sheet on your pad. Across the top write "All the *Practical* Reasons I Haven't Been Able to Write." List everything you can think of: My job takes too much time; I have to go to the health club; I have children; My classes have to come first; My apartment's too noisy. . . . Some of these will be carried over from your first list. Others will be new. That doesn't matter, just get them all down.

Stop and do the list now, before you go on to the next paragraph.

Okay, done? Good. Now, cross out what you first wrote at the top of the page, and above it write: "Decoy List." That's what they are, decoys. The only real reason for not writing is the *decision* not to write, motivated chiefly by Perfectionism and the Baggage Train. Tear the page off, fold it in half. Fold it again. Stand up, walk to the nearest wastebasket, and drop it in: You're all done with that stuff. You know now that there is no such thing as writer's block or any reason that can truly prevent you from writing.

2.
SEEING IT RIGHTLY.

By now it's clear that what we call block stems almost entirely from what we believe or fear—what we *think* to be true, what we *think* will happen. These thoughts, or beliefs, operate for the most part in our subconscious. How did we acquire them? Basically, we were programmed, by ourselves and others. In its earliest forms, most of this programming took place when we were quite young—before our intelligence was sufficiently developed to be of much help to us in evaluating what was coming in. It happened in three different ways:

1. We processed various bits of information about ourselves and the world and drew a conclusion.

2. Someone told us something about ourselves or the world and we accepted it as true.

3. We overhead others talking about us or the world and we believed what they said.

So early on, before we could even begin to understand what such statements meant, we accepted as true such distortions as:
"Life is tough."
"I'm not worth much."
"I have to please people to be liked."
"You have to suffer to get ahead."
"It's immoral to enjoy yourself while others are suffering."
And all the rest.

As we grew older, we modified or elaborated these to fit new situations. "I'm not worth much" may have become "Nobody is interested in what I have to say." "Life is tough" might have worked into "Writing is pain." We then proceeded to live, feel, and behave according to these beliefs as if they were universal truths instead of what they really are, simply the distorted judgments and opinions of others, programmed into our subconscious.

This negative programming has a crippling and destructive effect upon us. It needs to be counteracted. Taking action in the face of it, which the techniques in this part of the book will enable you to do, helps quite a bit. Another, and very effective way, is to assume control of the programming ourselves, through the use of affirmations.

To affirm something is to declare it positively or firmly, to maintain it to be true. The word derives from the Latin *affirmare*, which means to fix in place, to make solid, to make strong or healthy.

An affirmation is a strong positive thought you implant in your subconscious with the intention of producing a healthy change in your attitudes and perceptions. Affirmations are much more than simple positive thinking. They are specific and powerful vehicles of change, and if systematically employed they can and do bring about such internal change, which, by consequence, leads inevitably to external change.

It doesn't matter whether or not you believe your affirmations. Even if you find them absurd and incredible, your subconscious will, in time, begin to accept them.

The best way to work with them is to write them out. (This is the only process in the book designed to be undertaken at a later date.) Here's how you do it: Draw a line down a sheet of paper lengthwise. Write the positive affirmation on the left. As soon as you do, jot down on the right the first thought that comes to mind. This response column is important. It allows your subconscious to raise all the objections it wants, to get the junk out of its system.

Write the affirmation five times in the first person "I." Then five times in the second person, using your own name. Then five times in the third person, using your own name. Using the three voices—first, second, and third person—gets this new attitude into your subconscious in the same way the old distorted ones entered: through what you told yourself, what others told you, and what you heard others say.

The process looks like this:

Writing is easy and fun for me.	That's a crock!
Writing is easy and fun for me.	Blow it out your nose.
Writing is easy and fun for me.	Right, like root canal.
Writing is easy and fun for me.	Tell it to the marines.
Writing is easy and fun for me.	Yeah, sometimes.
Jerry, writing is easy and fun for you.	In a pig's eye.

Jerry, writing is easy and fun for you.	Sometimes.
Jerry, writing is easy and fun for you.	Your mama.
Jerry, writing is easy and fun for you.	Ho-hum.
Jerry, writing is easy and fun for you.	What am I, the village idiot?
Writing is easy and fun for Jerry.	Sure it is.
Writing is easy and fun for Jerry.	Okay, okay, already.
Writing is easy and fun for Jerry.	This is boring.
Writing is easy and fun for Jerry.	Maybe it is.
Writing is easy and fun for Jerry.	Uh-huh.

Here are a few affirmations people have used to strong effect:

I am never at a loss for words.

It's safe for me to take chances.

I now have lavishly abundant time for my writing.

I am a richly talented writer.

Everyone wants me to succeed.

The Universe gives me all the inspiration I need.

I am now ready to accept my talent fully and joyously.

The more I win, the better I feel about letting others win.

I now see success followed by greater success for me. My success is big, powerful, and irresistible.

Writing is my friend.

The more truthfully I write the more people like me

I now have more than enough knowledge to satisfy all my needs and desires.

It's okay for me to exceed my goals.

The more I prosper, the more I have to share with others.

I am now ready to accept all the joy and pleasure life has to offer me.

If you had a strong negative reaction to any of these—found them irrational, absurd, even horrifying—then they are precisely the ones you should start working with. A powerful negative response usually means that a given affirmation is colliding head-on with its opposite, with a distorted belief that's deeply entrenched in your subconscious. And those are the ones you most need to root out.

It's best to work with a single affirmation at a time. Write it out in the style just described once each day for ten to fourteen days. Be sure to use the response column. (You'll probably note that the negative responses become less violent after a few days and that some tentative positive ones begin to creep in. That's a sign that your subconscious is beginning to give up the ferocity of its initial resistance.) Then write it out a few more days without the response column, allowing it to sink in uncontested.

You can create your own affirmations too, tailoring them to specific needs. First, identify the negative statement. For example:

"I always get nervous and flustered when I sit down to write."
Then reverse it into its opposite, being careful to use only positive
language; don't phrase it in a way that *seems* positive but which
in fact either contains a negative subtext or invites negative association. "I never get nervous or flustered when I sit down to
write" is not very helpful. It contains negative words and elements
of struggle and denial.

Let's try again.

Negative statement: "I always get nervous and flustered when
I sit down to write."

Affirmation: "A literary challenge always brings out the best
in me."

Or: "The more I'm challenged, the happier and more confident I become."

Remember, your initial disbelief, or even revulsion toward the
affirmation, is irrelevant to its eventual impact. If you work with
it, it will begin to work for you. You can strengthen the process
by taking a few moments after waking and at intervals during the
day simply to say the affirmation out loud or silently to yourself
three or four times.

Many scoff when they first encounter the idea of affirmations.
So did I. But on the other hand, I eventually decided, a closed
mind has never been the hallmark of a functioning intelligence, and
it wouldn't cost me much to give it a try. So I did. Carefully,
privately—after all, I had a reputation of intellectual skepticism to
maintain. Today I employ affirmations regularly; I'm enough of a
pragmatist to use what works.

3.
GOALS.

For the final exercise in this chapter, turn to a fresh page on your pad. Across the top write: "Goals." What you're going to formulate here are *writing* goals, not marketing goals. And whether you meet them or not is irrelevant. Their only purpose is to help you establish a vision, to set up a series of road signs that help you keep going in the right direction.

Put down a heading: *Five Years*. Beneath it list five writing goals you would like to have accomplished by five years from now. That's a good chunk of time, with a lot of room. But be reasonable, taking into account your responsibilities and the demands on your time. What is reasonable for one person may be unreasonable for another, but the following are representative of what many people who work full time come up with.

1. Have written regularly.

2. Have finished two novels.

3. Have completed a collection of poetry.

4. Have written ten essays or features.

5. Have gone to three writers' conferences.

Professionals, and beginners with more time available to write, such as retired persons, usually formulate larger goals: to have completed five books, for example, instead of two. There is no right or wrong in this, only what is reasonable for you.

Beneath your five-year goals, write the heading: *One Year*. Now list five writing goals you would like to have accomplished by one year from now. The list might look something like this.

1. Have the outline and the first three chapters of a book finished.

2. Have written two short stories.

3. Have written one essay.

4. Have read two books a month—or two feature articles a week— of the kind I want to write.

5. Have worked steadily with affirmations.

Now write the heading: *One Month.* Beneath this list four writing goals you would like to have accomplished by one month from now. A typical list might be:

1. Have decided what I want to write.

2. Have subscribed to *Writer's Digest.*

3. Have met my writing schedule.

4. Have written the first draft of a short story or feature.

As you'll note, the larger the time frame, the larger the goal; conversely, the smaller the time frame, the smaller the goal. One of your five-year goals, for example, is to have finished two novels—but your goal for the coming month may be simply to decide what *kind* of novel you want to write. You begin with a definite vision of what you eventually want on the large scale, then reduce it into ever smaller goals as you approach nearer to today. This ensures that all of your actions, no matter how small, move you steadily toward your large-scale goals, which are much further off.

Remember, a goal is not something you *have* to achieve. It should be neither a lash on your back nor a mechanism of potential failure. It is simply a guideline, a signpost to help you keep moving in the right direction.

This brings to an end the soft techniques. Pause here for a minute or two. Set the book aside, stand up, and stretch. Take a couple of slow deep breaths. Shift your shoulders about or touch your toes. When you feel relaxed and clear, sit down, get comfortable, and begin reading again.

CHAPTER

13

FIRM TECHNIQUES

What gets a manuscript finished is steady progress, not fits and starts or grabbing hours when you can. The turtle wins the race every time. Crucial in this is a dependable writing schedule. So our first task in this chapter is to:

1.
ESTABLISH A WRITING SCHEDULE.

Schedules vary. Matthew Braun, a western writer, writes eight hours a day, five days a week. John Shearer, a novelist and children's book author—who is also a full-time photo editor at *The New York Times*—writes from 10 to 11:30 P.M., four nights a week, and two or three hours on Saturday. Lawrence Block, a mystery novelist, sequesters himself in a writer's colony or hotel room and writes nearly every waking hour, finishing a book in four or five weeks.

Each of these schedules is valid for the individual, but none is typical. The average full-time writer puts in four to four-and-a-half hours a day, five days a week; the average part-time writer puts in one to two hours a day, five or six days a week. Ordinarily, both write early. My own schedule is to write from 10 in the morning to 2 in the afternoon, Monday through Friday. When I'm working on revision, I might raise that by an hour to an hour and a half a day. Linda Lee, a magazine writer who has published three books and who is also a single mother with a full-time job, writes from 7 to 8:15 each weekday morning and from 9 to 11 on Saturday morning.

The first step in establishing a schedule is to determine how many hours a week are available for you to write. This is not the same as asking how much "free" time you have. There are more claims on your time than you think, including the important one of rest and relaxation, the need to socialize and have fun. Nearly everyone who is blocked has overestimated the time he or she can, or should, devote to writing. Writing is energy-intensive. Over-reaching invites burnout and block.

Take a moment here to reflect on the various aspects of your life: work, family, household, classes, other obligations. How many hours can you actually allocate to writing, and on what days?

To serve as models, here are two schedules I worked out with clients who were blocked. The first was a man who worked full time in television production and was the author of two books. He was divorced, and his teenage son lived with him. Because he didn't have to be in the office till 10:30 in the morning, his schedule was simple and straightforward, to write from 8:30 to 10,

Monday through Friday. The second was a student in Columbia University's Graduate Writing Program, who, in addition to attending classes, was a part-time proofreader. That made her week a patchwork of obligations we had to work around. Her schedule was to write from 9 to 10:30 Monday and Tuesday mornings, from 11 to noon on Wednesday, nothing on Thursday, from 4 to 5 P.M. on Friday, and from 9 to 11 A.M. on Saturday.

With these examples in mind, and remembering not to overextend yourself, set the book aside and draw up a schedule for yourself. This is a *preliminary* schedule. Before you make it final, you will need to read the next two topics. In Chapter 15 we'll be discussing an extremely potent technique through which to implement your schedule.

2.
IF POSSIBLE, WRITE FIRST THING IN THE MORNING.

By writing first thing in the morning, if you can, you take advantage of your clarity of mind and higher energy. The normal activities of the day will eventually drain your energy and blunt your mental faculties. It is possible to write at day's end, after job and other responsibilities have been acquitted, and some do. But you'll give yourself a significant advantage by sitting down to it when you are fresh. If there are major claims upon your morning, then try getting to bed an hour earlier, so you can get up an hour earlier and devote that time to your writing.

3.

DON'T PLAN TO WRITE ON WEEKENDS, IF YOU CAN AVOID IT.

Planning to use the weekend to write may seem a logical choice if you have a job or are in school. But most people who try it quickly come to resent having to "work" on their days off. In short order, they find excuses to avoid it, then stop altogether. That often causes guilt and self-disgust, which can lead directly to block. At the most, you should consider writing for no more than an hour or two on Saturday, preferably first thing in the morning, and then giving yourself the rest of the weekend off.

Now is the time to make your writing schedule final. While you do, keep in mind all the information in these first three sections. You shouldn't need more than a few minutes, working from your preliminary schedule. When you're done, pause, take a couple of breaths, relax, and then go on to the next topic.

4.

DRESS FOR THE OCCASION.

Don't stumble out of bed, make a cup of coffee, throw on a housecoat or yesterday's Levi's and sweatshirt, and sit down to write. Feel good about yourself. Shower, shave, and put on clean clothes first. Respect yourself and your writing. Begin with your hair washed, some basic makeup on if you wish, and wearing clothes in which you feel comfortable, self-cared for, and attractive. If you have to go to an office afterward, you might put on your dress shoes, suit pants and shirt, or skirt and blouse but wait until your writing period is over before donning your tie (if appropriate) and jacket.

5.
SEPARATE YOUR WRITING FROM THE REST OF YOUR DAY.

Before you begin your writing period, meditate or do a relaxation exercise. This makes an effective transition between your normal routines and your writing; it calms you, quiets other concerns, and prepares you to be fully present and focused when you begin to write. Meditation and relaxation techniques, if you are unfamiliar with them, usually can be learned at yoga centers, YMCAs, stress management courses offered by hospitals, or even through books and videotapes. There are many forms, and practically any one you like will do. Five to fifteen minutes are generally enough, depending on how busy or involved in other matters you've been. At the end of your writing period, meditate or do a relaxation exercise again. This helps you leave the writing behind, which is where it belongs, and provides a transition back into your other activities. If your normal schedule is tight, be sure to factor in this extra time. The beginning meditation or relaxation exercise is especially important if you are unable to write first thing in the morning.

6.
FORGET ABOUT WHETHER THE WORK IS GOOD, BAD, OR INDIFFERENT.

Forget about the quality of the work. Whether the last paragraph was brilliant or hopeless is irrelevant. It does not matter whether a reader would weep with joy or grimace with disgust over a metaphor; whether the correct spelling is j-u-d-g-e-m-e-n-t or j-u-d-g-m-e-n-t; whether you've split an infinitive—or if you have, whether that's fine here or not. Those are all questions for later, for revision. Your only job during your writing period is to put words on paper. That is a simple act. Keep it simple.

7.
IF YOU CAN, DO SOMETHING PLEASURABLE AFTER WRITING.

When you're done writing, take a walk, throw a stick for the dog, put some music on and dance, or do whatever else is fun. This helps your mind associate the act of writing with pleasure, which is a useful association. It also lubricates your reentry back into other routines.

8.
PAY YOURSELF FOR EACH DAY'S WRITING.

Writing is aesthetically and emotionally rewarding. But it's nice to be paid for it too. That, after all, is why professionals do it. So at the end of each writing day, if you'd like, pay yourself. Put five dollars or one dollar or whatever suits your finances into a jar or envelope. At the end of the week take the money out, put it in your wallet, and spend it on whatever will give you the most satisfaction. It's your money, you've earned it.

9.
SELECT CRITICS OR CONFIDANTS CAREFULLY.

Be careful to whom you show your work. Even close friends may
have their own agendas, and respond from those, consciously or
unconsciously, under the guise of giving you objective feedback. It
is usually best to restrict your critics and confidants to no more
than two people. Ideally, they should be in some way qualified to
comment on a piece of writing, if only by the fact that they read
a lot. And they should be people who you are certain wish you
well and have your best interests at heart.

This brings to a close the Firm Techniques. Pause here and look
back over the headings in this chapter to impress them into your
mind. Then set the book down. Stretch. Breathe. Relax. And
move on to the next chapter.

CHAPTER

14

HARDCORE TECHNIQUES

You have made tremendous progress since you began this book. You understand the nature and source of block. You've learned a number of effective techniques to use in demolishing it. You are very nearly at the point of being able to write steadily and reliably. The techniques in this and the next chapter will give you the rest of the tools you need to free yourself forever.

1.
THE PLACE TO WRITE.

You need a place to write—one that you use strictly for writing and nothing else. Not to study, not to pay bills, not to write letters or perform any other activity in. When you sit down there, your mind should associate it with only one act, writing.

I have had many places to write, as many as I have had places to live. My favorite was a room twenty feet long by twenty feet wide on the second floor of an outbuilding close to my house in the Catskill Mountains, where I lived during the 1970s. A large bay window overlooked a meadow, with woods and a mountain behind. In an adjoining room was my library; there were additional bookcases in the writing room itself. I worked at a large old oak desk, facing the windows. At dusk, during the late summer and fall, deer would come out of the woods and move slowly across the meadow to forage beneath the apple trees near the house. It was a good place to write.

But so have been all the others I created: the gray metal desk in a college dormitory room I intuitively used for nothing but that purpose, studying in a chair or on my bed or in the library; the narrow "maid's" room I converted into my office in an apartment on Manhattan's Upper West Side, where I lived with my wife and children in the late 1960s; the corner of a Manhattan studio apartment in the early 1980s, in which I had a small desk custom built, and behind it positioned a filing cabinet and mounted shelves for my reference books.

Ideally, anyone who writes will have a separate room to devote strictly to his or her writing. But most situations are usually not ideal. How then does one create a place to write when space is limited—say, a tiny studio apartment? Anywhere can be transformed into such a place. That is as much a psychological reality as a physical one. A kitchen table can be converted into your place to write—for the duration of your writing period, which is all that is necessary—by stripping it clean of place mats, bowl of fruit, napkin holder, salt and pepper shakers, and every other usual item, then by placing on it only those objects you will use during your writing: typewriter or computer, note pad, pens, and books. It has ceased to be a kitchen table. It has become your place to write.

My current apartment is a three-and-a-half room duplex. One room is devoted almost exclusively to writing. Occasionally I sit and chat with a friend there rather than in the living room, and I do pay bills at my desk and answer correspondence there. And often, because of the layout of the apartment and my other activities, books, magazines, or letters will have been placed on my desk by the end of the night, even a bag of laundry, or a hat and a pair of gloves. My final act, before I go upstairs to bed, is to clear the desk of everything not directly related to tomorrow's writing, even if that means nothing more than transferring it to the couch to await final disposition. This ensures that when I come down in the morning to begin my writing period, my desk has on it nothing but what I need for my writing and is indeed my place to write.

Having a place to write is vital. And anyone, regardless of circumstances, can create one. Doing so should be a priority.

2.
HAVE ALL YOUR TOOLS AT HAND.

Equip yourself with everything you will need before you begin your writing period. In addition to your computer and disks, or typewriter and paper, or yellow pad and pencils, make sure that you have note pads, reference books, (dictionary and thesaurus if you're on revision) interview tapes and player, research files, and anything else you'll want. This further solidifies your place to write and eliminates having to break your train of thought to go get something. It is perfectly all right to take a break when you *want* to, but it is annoying to *have* to.

3.
YOUR WRITING TIME IS SACROSANCT.

The time you have set aside to write is sacrosanct. It is not flex time. It is not to be used to fit in a dentist's appointment, pick up the dry cleaning, solace an unhappy friend, or take the cat to the vet. It is your writing time, and it is inviolable. It takes precedence over *everything*.

Unplug your telephone or turn the bell off. If you have an answering machine, do *not* monitor calls. You can check them later. In more than twenty years of writing I have never suffered even a minor loss to my career or social life by not answering the phone during working hours. The same goes for the doorbell.

If you live with family or others, explain to them the importance—the need—for you to have this period to yourself, free from interruption and distraction. If you can, schedule your writing time during hours when you would normally have the house to yourself. In any case, you have the right, and the responsibility, to tell the children not to play music loudly while you're writing or your spouse not to wander in to show you this terrifically funny thing he or she just found in the paper. Your writing time is sacrosanct.

4.
START TODAY'S WORK WITH SOME OF YESTERDAY'S WORK.

It's easier to get a writing period underway if you begin a bit behind yourself rather than with the first new sentence you have to write. Back up a page or so and start editing—lightly, without trying to produce final copy—until you reach the point where you stopped yesterday. Then just continue with the new text. This eases you back into the piece and starts the flow again with a minimum of effort. I nearly always edit the previous page when beginning the new day's work. On Monday, when I've been away from writing for two full days, I usually edit the previous five pages to smooth my way in.

5.
AUTOMATIC WRITING.

If you find yourself stalled, spend five minutes in automatic writing, the kind you did in Chapter 2, when you began with the sentence "I am years gone from my family and miles away." As you did then, simply keep your pen moving, or your fingers moving on the keyboard, putting down one word after the other.

This writing doesn't have to relate at all to what you're working on. Whatever comes out is just fine. Toward the end, steer it in the direction of your work, something like "If I were writing the book now I'd probably be talking about how John used to live on a farm and how when he was maybe nine, ten years old dust motes in the hayloft floating in the sunlight along with the heat of a late summer afternoon used to be a transcendent state for him." Then move back into the actual piece. Put down anything at all for a minute or two and take it from there.

6.

SWITCH YOUR MODE OF COMPOSITION.

If you're stuck, switch to another mode of composition for an hour, a day, or a couple of days: from computer to typewriter, or from typewriter to pen and paper. If you normally write with pen and paper, change the color of the ink or paper. This breaks the chain, injects novelty, and helps you approach the work with a new perspective.

7.

RELAX.

Remember: Peaks and valleys are normal. It is normal to be stalled for a few minutes, to stare at the screen and think, "Oh, Jesus, what would she say here?" or "How on earth does this tie in with his allergy?" If you find yourself growing tense or locked up at such moments, take a couple of breaths, relax, remind yourself of Perfectionism, Fear, and the Baggage Train, and then just write the next sentence or paragraph, no matter what it sounds like.

8.

WHEN YOUR WRITING TIME IS OVER, IT'S OVER.

Whether you write from 10 A.M. till 11 A.M., from 9 in the morning till 9 at night, or on any other schedule, when your writing time is over, it's over. Set a kitchen timer or an alarm clock to signal the end of your scheduled period—and when the alarm goes off, *stop*. You can finish the sentence on which you're working and write a note to yourself to indicate where you're going with this paragraph or scene, but that's it, no more. We'll have some further things to say about this in the next chapter, but for now, simply know that it is important not to exceed the boundaries of your writing schedule.

It's time to pause again, take a couple of breaths, stretch, and relax. When you have, go on to the next chapter.

CHAPTER

15

THE ATOM BOMB

This is the big one. Backed by your knowledge of what causes block, and supported by the other techniques you've learned, this is guaranteed to blow writer's block right off the face of your earth. It is:

THE SHORT-TIME METHOD

The Short-Time Method, though astonishingly powerful, is simple to execute. This is how you do it: When you find yourself running into serious trouble or grinding to a halt, when you sense that the onset of block may be imminent, *immediately* and *severely* curtail the length of your writing day. Cut it down by at least 75 percent.

What! But I'll never get anything done. I'll fall even further behind. Jesus, I've got to work even harder to make up for what I've *already* lost!

Dead wrong, my friend. That's the voice of Perfectionism, Fear, and the Baggage Train. Hurling yourself against the wall of block, trying to break through by sheer force of will, doesn't work. You've done that before: driven yourself, berated yourself, promised to reward yourself, begged, pleaded, lashed, and threatened yourself. And all you ever did was fail, again and again, and the block grew stronger, and the agony increased, and you grew progressively more depressed, despondent, hopeless, and the block got even worse.

All that is over. Pause here, and take two deep breaths. Let your body relax. Smile. Smile again. You know what writer's block is now and where it comes from. You know that it is an illusion, that there is no such thing. And with this, the Short-Time Method, you have all the concepts and techniques you need never to be victimized by it again. So relax and enjoy it.

The key, as we said, is to *restrict severely* the length of your writing period. If that is normally four hours, then permit yourself to write no more than one hour. If your normal writing period is one hour, then permit yourself to write no more than fifteen minutes. Observe this restriction scrupulously. It must be *absolute*. Set your timer or clock for precisely one hour, or fifteen minutes, or whatever else is appropriate, and when it goes off, *stop*. Do not write for even ten seconds more, no matter what the circumstances or how much you want to. Make *no* exceptions.

Note the element of permission here. You are not forcing yourself to work for an hour, you are *permitting* yourself to work for *no more* than an hour.

I have used the Short-Time Method many, many times over my career. I revert to it the moment I become aware that the trouble I'm having with a piece has moved beyond a normal level of difficulty and frustration and is approaching block. Here's how I work it, over a period of four to six weeks:

Since my normal writing day is four hours, I cut that down to one. For the entire first week, I permit myself to work no more than one hour a day. I'm confident that if I forget about results, if I discard Perfectionism and the Baggage Train, I can perform the simple act of putting words on paper for a single hour. (A few times, still having difficulty, I cut that down to half an hour. If necessary, though it's unlikely you'll have to, be prepared to cut your writing day to no more than five minutes: Anyone can perform the simple act of putting words on paper for five minutes.)

The first result is nearly always a sense of relief. I don't have to sit in my chair facing potential agony for four hours. Further, I won't even *allow* myself to spend more than an hour there, even if I want to or think that I ought to. The second result, inevitably, is that within a day or two—usually not more than three or four—when the alarm surprises me, I think: "Hey, I know where to go with this paragraph. Let me have just a couple of minutes to finish it." But I don't give myself those couple of minutes. I stop, allowing only three or four seconds to type myself a note indicating where I want to go tomorrow, something like "So she buys the shoes, but doesn't like them." I finish the week thus.

The second week, I permit myself to write no more than an hour and a half a day; the third week, no more than two hours; the fourth week, no more than two-and-three-quarter hours; the fifth week, no more than three-and-a-half hours. By the sixth week, I am back up to a full working day.

Early in the process—often by the end of the first week—I begin to grow frustrated by the restriction. Increasingly, I want to exceed it. Before long I become impatient, eager, even hungry to plunge back in to full writing days. Frequently I don't even complete the six-week period, am back to a normal schedule by the fourth week. But I have long experience with working this method; I strongly suggest that you stay with the six-week form until you do too.

If your normal writing day is one hour, cut it to fifteen minutes the first week. Permit yourself no more than twenty minutes the second week, thirty the third week, forty the fourth week, and fifty the fifth week. In the sixth week, allow yourself to return to a full hour. Anyone can create a Short-Time Schedule by modifying these examples according to the number of hours in his or her own normal writing day.

It is vital that you adhere to the restriction scrupulously. Do not allow yourself to exceed your limit for even a single day. And do not decide at some point along the way that you're already so filled with enthusiasm and vitality that you won't bother completing the schedule. To return to full days before you are really ready, even if that *feels* right, is to court block again.

The Short-Time Method is also a potent way to implement a new writing schedule or to reenter writing after an extended absence, such as a long vacation. Trying to move overnight from a standstill into a full writing schedule is often to overreach and set up the potential for block.

In the late 1980s, because of responsibilities that required a stable income, I went to work for *The New York Times* as an editor for a year and a half. Since I hadn't been in an office in more than twenty years, I decided to take a year off from my own writing. And I did. When, twelve months later, I began to write again, I did so by putting in fifteen minutes each workday morning during the first week, with half an hour on Saturday. In the second week, I raised that to twenty minutes a morning, with forty on Saturday. I went to half an hour a morning in the third week, an hour on Saturday; and in the fourth week to forty-five minutes, with an hour and a half on Saturday. By the fifth week I was writing at a full schedule: one hour each morning before I left for work, and two hours on Saturday.

When I left the paper several months later to write full time again, I began by restricting myself to an hour and a half each morning, five days a week, for the first week. In the second week I raised that to two hours a day, and by the fifth week I was up to my normal four-hour writing day.

Did I need to approach my return to writing so conservatively? Probably not. It's likely I could have doubled those starting times, and maybe there was no need to restrict myself at all. Maybe. But the point is, that coming off a full year of not writing, I was working productively from the very first day and within weeks writing at full capacity, without experiencing anything that even remotely resembled block.

If, after you have successfully moved yourself back to a full writing schedule, you find that you are still uncomfortable or straining too much, you may be confusing the normal difficulties of writing with some inadequacy in yourself or impending block. Relax. Remember, the words don't always flow. Writing requires effort, just like any other art or profession, and sometimes it's plain hard work.

Check yourself for Perfectionism or the Baggage Train again. Be sure you're not neglecting the other techniques. Consider the possibility that the schedule you have set may be too demanding. Look at it again in light of your other responsibilities and obligations, your need for rest and recreation. Be prepared to scale it back, if necessary, to something that is more realistic.

Finally, and again: No matter what your schedule, it should *always* contain a specified stopping time. Stick to that time, despite the days on which you are aflame with inspiration and *know* you can write for another hour, two, three, or through the night in a white heat. That can be done. But shortly you will find yourself exhausted, depleted, and struggling to meet your normal working schedule. What gets a manuscript finished is steady daily work, not white heats.

16

MUNDIS'S PERSONAL BIGGIES

I have used and do use all of the concepts and techniques in this book in my own work, and on a regular basis. In fact, I brought most of them into play while writing this book itself. You will prefer, or find most helpful, some more than others; but none should be neglected: It is in concert, as a coherent system, that they have their greatest impact. And practiced thus, they will not fail to demolish writer's block and enable you to establish a reliable and productive working schedule.

Because the people I work with often ask, here are the concepts and techniques I find particularly effective with myself:

1. Block is unreal. It stems almost entirely from Perfectionism, Fear, and the Baggage Train.

2. The Place to Write.

3. Edit some of yesterday's work as a way in to today's work.

4. The Short-Time Method.

Writing is the simple act of putting words on paper. For some it is an avocation, for others, a profession. For all it is at once difficult and pleasurable, a source of joy and a source of frustration.

Writer's block, that most feared and cruelly painful state, is wholly unnecessary. What you have done this afternoon, by reading this book and working the exercises within it, is to have demolished block and liberated yourself from it forever. If you absorb these concepts into your consciousness, and work with these techniques on a daily basis, you need never fear or be crippled by block again. I wish for you happiness and pleasure in your work and satisfaction and success in whatever you wish to do with it. Godspeed.

A FINAL NOTE

I always enjoy hearing from readers but can't always respond to everyone or in detail. Enclosing a stamped, self-addressed envelope helps. Know that even if I'm unable to get back to you, I'm grateful for your letter.

When responsibilities permit, I'm available for personal consultation or group seminars.

I can be reached by writing to:

Jerrold Mundis
P.O. Box 30242
Port Authority Station
New York, N.Y. 10011